X-Sports

SNOWBOARDING

BY ERIC PRESZLER

CONSULTANT:
MICHAEL MALLON
PRO COACH

Capstone
press

Mankato, Minnesota

Edge Books are published by Capstone Press
151 Good Counsel Drive, P.O. Box 669, Mankato, Minnesota 56002
www.capstonepress.com

Library of Congress Cataloging-in-Publication Data
Preszler, Eric.
    Snowboarding / by Eric Preszler.
    p. cm.—(Edge books. X-sports)
    Includes bibliographical references and index.
    ISBN 0-7368-2713-7 (hardcover)
    1. Snowboarding—Juvenile literature. I. Title. II. Series.
GV857.S57P74 2005
796.939—dc22   2004000514

Summary: Discusses the sport of snowboarding, including gear needed, tricks, and
    famous snowboarders.

Editorial Credits

Tom Adamson, editor; Jason Knudson, designer and illustrator; Jo Miller,
    photo researcher; Eric Kudalis, product planning editor

Photo Credits

AP/Wide World Photos/Arno Balzarini, 28
Corbis/Duomo/Chris Trotman, 11; David Stoecklein, 15, 17;
    Reuters NewMedia Inc., 21
Gallup Photography Inc./Mark Gallup, 9 (top), 13, 19 (both), 20
Getty Images/Jeb Jacobsohn, 9 (bottom), 22; Mike Powell, 27
Mercury Press/Isaac Hernandez, 14
Sherman Poppen, 6
SportsChrome Inc./Rob Tringali, cover
Unicorn Stock Photos/Novastock, 5

1 2 3 4 5 6 09 08 07 06 05 04

TABLE OF CONTENTS

CHAPTER 1

SNOWBOARDING

The snowboarder balances high on a large mountain ridge. He gazes down at the powdery snow. He slowly shifts his weight downhill. He drops the nose of the board over the edge.

In no time, he is gliding down the mountainside. The board carves through the powder. It launches snow in the air like waves. He approaches a large drift. The rider bends his knees and prepares for takeoff. In one fluid motion, he is spinning through the air.

EARLY SNOWBOARDS

Snowboarding has been popular since its beginnings in the 1960s. Skiing, skateboarding, and surfing all shaped snowboarding.

LEARN ABOUT:

- The Snurfer
- Jake Burton Carpenter
- Snowboarding styles

Some snowboarders like to catch air in fine powder.

Snurfers were early versions of the snowboard.

One of the earliest snowboards was a toy called the Snurfer. Sherman Poppen developed the Snurfer in 1965. He bolted two skis together and attached a rope to the front. The rider slid down the hill holding the rope.

Jake Burton Carpenter developed the modern snowboard. When Burton was a teenager, he had a Snurfer. He experimented with it to make it faster. He added bindings so he had more control. He realized snowboards could be more than just a toy.

Burton began making and selling his own snowboards. In the late 1970s, he started his company, Burton Snowboards. Today, Burton Snowboards sells more snowboards and equipment than any other company.

BINDINGS

Snowboards in the 1970s were still missing one important detail. Many snowboards didn't have safe bindings. Some snowboards didn't have bindings at all. In the early 1980s, snowboard fan Jeff Grell invented a new binding system. It kept riders' feet attached safely to the board.

SNOWBOARDING STYLES

Some snowboarders like to catch big air. Others race in competitions. Many riders participate in more than one style.

Freestyle snowboarding includes slopestyle and halfpipe events. In slopestyle, riders perform tricks off jumps and on rails. They also do tricks off natural obstacles. Some riders do tricks in halfpipes. Halfpipes are U-shaped. They look like half of a pipe. Riders catch big air and do spins and grabs above halfpipes. Freestyle riders impress crowds and the judges with their tricks.

An alpine snowboarder is either a racer or an alpine freerider. The racer's main goal is speed and precision. Alpine racers carve through gates. Freeriders ride on groomed slopes.

Freeriders combine alpine, freestyle, and slopestyle. They make use of the full mountain. Freeriding isn't a competition. It's just for fun.

EDGE FACT

In 1983, at least 90 percent of U.S. ski areas banned snowboarding.

Snowboarders catch big air above the halfpipe.

In slopestyle, riders do tricks on rails, jumps, and other obstacles.

CHAPTER 2
SNOWBOARDING GEAR

A snowboarder needs more than a snowboard. Boots and bindings should match a rider's style and size. Riders often use goggles and durable gloves. Some snowboarders wear helmets to prevent injury.

Snowboarding is a winter sport. Riders need warm clothes. Clothing should be worn in layers that can be taken off or put on depending on temperature. Cotton clothes should be avoided because they dry slowly.

LEARN ABOUT:
- Boards
- Boots
- Bindings

Snowboarders need to use gear that will keep them warm and safe.

FREERIDE GEAR

A freerider uses a board between the sizes of the alpine and freestyle board. The board is usually longer than a freestyle board but shorter than an alpine board.

Many freeriders use a soft boot, but it may not be as flexible as a freestyle boot. Freeride bindings are usually the same as freestyle bindings.

FREESTYLE GEAR

Freestyle and slopestyle riders use the shortest boards. Short, wide, flexible boards help riders perform tricks. A freestyle board is also lightweight.

EDGE FACT

In alpine snowboarding, making a precision turn without skidding is called carving. Alpine is sometimes called freecarving.

Freeriding boards help riders cut sharp turns.

Freestyle boards are flexible so riders can do spins and grabs.

Freestyle riders use soft boots that allow flexibility. The boards' bindings have high plastic backs for support and added control. Straps and buckles hold the boot in the binding.

ALPINE GEAR

Alpine riders use firmer and narrower boards than other styles. These boards help them turn sharply and quickly. Alpine boards are longer than other snowboards. They may be as long as

79 inches (200 centimeters). The boards' tails are usually cut straight across. The noses are slightly curved upward.

Alpine boots and bindings are stiffer like those used by skiers. Stiffer bindings give the rider greater control. Riders need control as they cut sharp angles on turns.

Freeriders sometimes touch the snow with one hand.

CHAPTER 3

SNOWBOARDING MOVES

Snowboarders ride on the boards either regular foot or goofy foot. Regular foot riders have their left foot forward. Goofy foot riders keep their right foot forward.

BASIC TRICKS

The ollie is a basic trick that helps riders get big air. While hitting a jump, the rider bends the front knee and shifts weight toward the back leg. The nose of the board comes up. The rider then straightens the front leg and shifts weight back to the center of the board.

LEARN ABOUT:

- Method grab
- McTwist
- Boardercross

A goofy foot rider has the right foot forward.

Many beginners start with a basic trick called the 180. The 180 is a half spin in the air. Riders start this trick with an ollie. Riders then twist the body in the air and land facing the opposite direction. When snowboarders land riding backwards, it's called riding fakie.

The method grab is another trick that beginners can master. In this trick, riders start with an ollie. They then grab the board near their front foot on the heel edge.

For added style, riders will bone out their tricks. Riders straighten the leg opposite the grab while throwing their free hand in the air.

Many basic tricks are part of more difficult tricks. For example, the 180 becomes a 360 when the rider spins all the way around. Riders also add flips to the basic spins and grabs.

ADVANCED TRICKS

The frontside air to fakie allows riders to catch big air. Riders glide up the halfpipe wall forward. They catch as much air as they can. They then land riding fakie. This move can include any type of grab.

Riders grab the heel edge for a method grab.

Freestyle riders do spins in the air.

19

The McTwist is a popular halfpipe move.

The Superman front flip is an exciting advanced trick. Riders fly off a large jump. They stretch out like Superman. To perform the flip, riders throw their arms down while tucking their feet. Riders keep their knees bent as they land.

Skateboarder Mike McGill made the McTwist famous. Snowboarders began doing the trick at slopes and halfpipes. The McTwist is a 540-degree rotation and a grab. The rider lands riding forward.

COMPETITIONS

Parallel giant slalom is a timed race. Riders make quick turns around gates. Two riders race against each other. They then switch sides. The winner is the one who has the best overall time. That rider moves on to the next round.

Parallel giant slalom is an intense downhill race.

Many riders race at the same time in the boardercross event.

Other snowboarding events include halfpipe, slopestyle, and boardercross. Riders perform a series of tricks in the halfpipe competition. Judges give scores to riders. The riders who perform their tricks the best get the highest scores. The slopestyle competition is a course full of jumps, rails, picnic tables, and other obstacles. Judges reward riders for stylish tricks and big air. The boardercross event is a race. It gets its name from motocross, a dirt bike racing event. Boardercross racers speed down a mountain course with banked turns and jumps.

EDGE FACT

The top halfpipe snowboarders can do a 1080. This move is three complete spins.

HOW TO DO A MCTWIST

1. The rider launches off the halfpipe ramp.

2. The rider grabs the toe edge of the board with the front hand.

3. The rider begins the rotation.

4. The rider keeps
   spinning to
   complete one
   and one-half turns.

5. The rider looks for
   the ramp and lands
   riding forward.

CHAPTER 4

FAMOUS SNOWBOARDERS

Snowboarding is still a new sport. The sport's inventors and new stars are helping to keep snowboarding popular.

SHAUN PALMER

Shaun Palmer competes in many snowboarding styles. He has competed in halfpipe, alpine, freestyle, and boardercross. He also competes in skiing, mountain biking, and motocross.

Palmer started snowboarding in 1982. He is a five-time World Champion. He also won the X Games boardercross event several times.

LEARN ABOUT:
- Shaun Palmer
- Tom Sims
- Michele Taggart

Shaun Palmer competes in many snowboarding styles, including boardercross.

Michele Taggart has been a top snowboarder for many years.

TOM SIMS

In 1963, Tom Sims changed his skateboard into a snowboard. He wanted to ride the streets during winter. The board he created was only 35 inches (89 centimeters) long.

Sims Snowboards are popular today. Sims' company helped start freestyle snowboarding. In 1983, the company held the first contest to have a halfpipe event. The contest was the World Snowboarding Championships at Lake Tahoe, California.

MICHELE TAGGART

Michele Taggart originally excelled in snow sports as a skier. It didn't take her long to become a great snowboarder. She won her first snowboard contest after snowboarding only three times.

Taggart has won more freestyle and alpine events than any other female rider. She recovered from a leg injury to win the World Cup halfpipe event in 1998. She also competed in the 1998 Olympics in Nagano, Japan. Taggart won the gold medal at the 1999 X Games in halfpipe.

GLOSSARY

bindings (BINDE-ingz)—straps and buckles that attach snowboarders' feet to the board

carve (KARV)—to make sharp turns on a snowboard without skidding

gate (GATE)—a narrow pole with a flag attached; slalom racers carve around gates in the parallel giant slalom event.

grab (GRAB)—a move in which the rider holds the board with one or both hands

halfpipe (HAF-pipe)—a U-shaped ramp with high walls; freestyle riders use halfpipes to do tricks.

nose (NOHZ)—the front end of a snowboard

tail (TAYL)—the back end of a snowboard

READ MORE

Barr, Matt, and Chris Moran. *Snowboarding.* Extreme Sports. Minneapolis: Lerner, 2004.

Brown, Gillian C. P. *Snowboarding.* X-treme Outdoors. New York: Children's Press, 2003.

Hedlund, Stephanie F. *Snowboarding.* X-treme Sports. Edina, Minn.: Abdo, 2003.

INTERNET SITES

FactHound offers a safe, fun way to find Internet sites related to this book. All of the sites on FactHound have been researched by our staff.

Here's how:

1. Visit *www.facthound.com*
2. Type in this special code **0736827137** for age-appropriate sites. Or enter a search word related to this book for a more general search.
3. Click on the **Fetch It** button.

FactHound will fetch the best sites for you!

INDEX